Cute Guys!

Coloring Book - Volume Two

A grown-up coloring book for ANYONE who loves cute guys!

Illustrations by Chayne Avery

Layout & Design by Russell Garcia

Be sure to follow or even post pictures of your finished pages on the **CuteGuys! Facebook page:** www.facebook.com/CuteGuysColoringBooks

All images copyright ©2016 Chayne Avery. All rights reserved. No part of this publication may be reproduced, distributed, or transmitted in any form or by any means, including photocopying, recording, or other electronic or mechanical methods, without the prior written permission of the author, except in the case of images embodied in critical reviews and certain other noncommercial uses permitted by copyright law.

For permission requests or any other correspondence, write to the artists at: ChayRussArt@gmail.com

Scribble Page

Use this page to test your art supplies before you dive into coloring the guys!

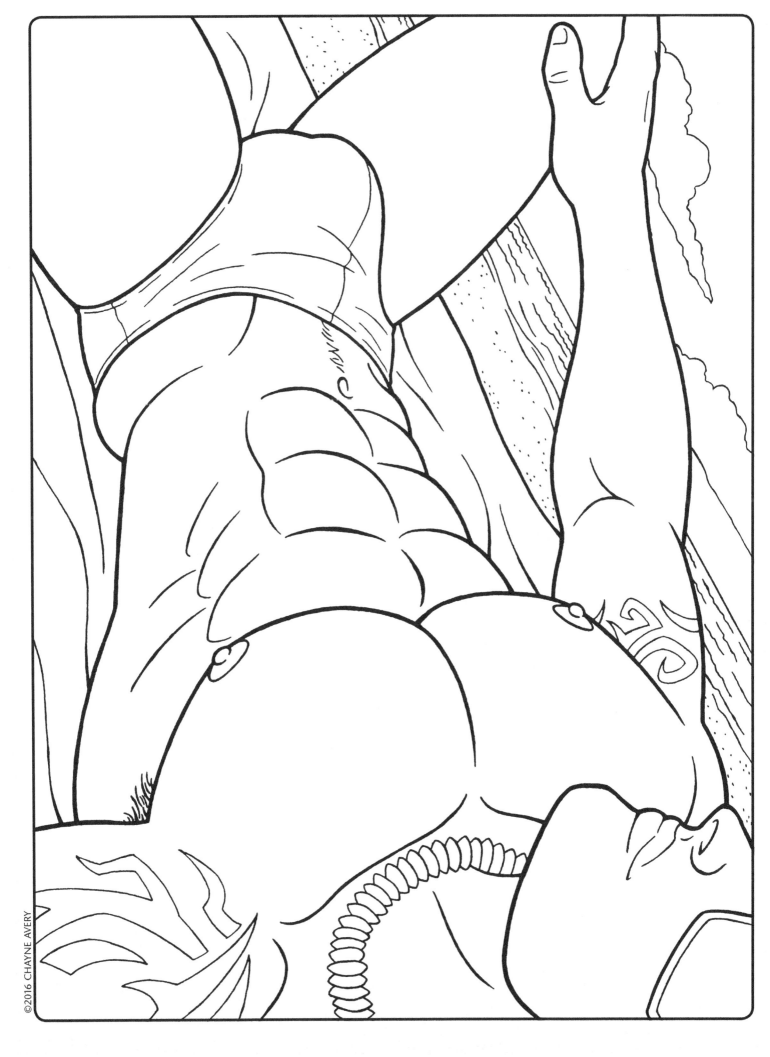

Made in the USA
Coppell, TX
02 May 2020